Everton

THE OFFICIAL
EVERTON
FOOTBALL CLUB
ANNUAL 2012

Written by Darren Griffiths

A Grange Publication

© 2011. Published by Grange Communications Ltd., Edinburgh, under licence from Everton Football Club. Printed in the EU.

Photographs © Everton Football Club

ISBN 978-1-908221-24-7

£7.99

CONTENTS

MEET

IT TOOK MORE THAN A HEAD INJURY
TO KEEP HIM OUT OF THE ACTION!

MOYES ON THE BALL AT
SHREWSBURY

IN ACTION IN SCOTLAND FO
DUNFERMLINE ATHLETIC

THE BOSS

David Moyes hasn't always been the manager of Everton Football Club!

Some of the younger readers may think he has – but the 'gaffer' was also a player who made over 500 appearances as a fearless centre-half.

He started his career at Glasgow Celtic, with whom he played in the European Cup and also won a Scottish Premier League winners' medal.

From Celtic he later played for Cambridge United, Bristol City, Shrewsbury, Dunfermline Athletic, Hamilton Academicals and Preston North End.

During his career, Moyes netted over 50 goals, which is a terrific figure for a defender.

It was whilst at Preston that he got involved first in coaching and then as the manager – with great success.

Everton came calling for him in March 2002 and he's been with us ever since...

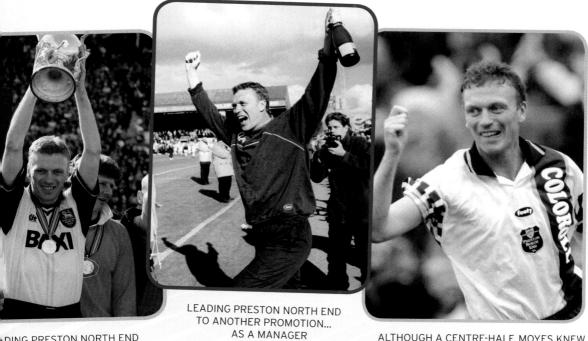

LEADING PRESTON NORTH END TO ANOTHER PROMOTION... AS A MANAGER

...DING PRESTON NORTH END PROMOTION...AS A PLAYER

ALTHOUGH A CENTRE-HALF, MOYES KNEW WHERE THE BACK OF THE NET WAS!

TOP TEN FROM TEN-ELEVEN

Here's our selection of the Top Ten highlights from the 2010/11 season...

1 FERGIE-TIME HORROR FOR UNITED!
11 September

Manchester United were leading 3-1 at Goodison Park as the 90th minute approached. Sir Alex must have thought the points were in the bag as stoppage time commenced but a Tim Cahill goal gave Everton hope and then, incredibly, a Mikel Arteta equaliser almost took the Goodison roof off! Unbelievably, The Toffees then launched another attack but the referee, Martin Atkinson, stopped them in their tracks with the final whistle.

2 DERBY DELIGHT!
17 October

Merseyside derby matches are traditionally feisty affairs but this one was a thoroughly comfortable victory for David Moyes' men. From the moment that Seamus Coleman danced to the by-line before setting

up Tim Cahill for the 34th minute opening goal, the outcome was hardly in doubt. Four minutes into the second half, Mikel Arteta made it 2-0 and there was no way back for Liverpool.

3 BLUES ARE CITY SLICKERS
20 December

Everton have a great record against Manchester City in recent seasons and they were off to a flyer in this one when Tim Cahill scored after just four minutes. The Toffees played some lovely football in the first-half and on 18 minutes it was 2-0 when Leighton Baines curled in a terrific shot past Joe Hart. Everton were reduced to 10 men on the hour when Victor Anichebe was sent off and with 18 minutes left Phil Jagielka accidentally deflected the ball into

his own net but a brave performance by the Blues earned three more points.

4 SEAMUS WINS HIS SPURS
5 January

Champions League-chasing Tottenham Hotspur were put to the sword on another memorable Goodison evening under floodlights. Once again Everton got off to a flying start with Louis Saha smashing the ball into the net from outside the box after just three minutes. The lead didn't last long though and Rafael van der Vaart levelled eight minutes later. It was a fine game and it was sealed by a diving header from Seamus Coleman in the 75th minute.

5 KING LOUIS THE FOURTH!
5 February

A good old fashioned game of football at Goodison Park against Blackpool in the pouring rain ended with Everton edging an 8-goal thriller! The star of the show was undoubtedly Louis Saha who plundered four goals for Everton – one in the first half and three in the second. Jermaine Beckford also got involved by scoring

the other goal.

6 BLUES WIN BRIDGE SHOOT-OUT!
19 February

Trailing 1-0 in the FA Cup 4th Round with one minute of extra time to play, Everton were awarded a free kick just outside the penalty area. The 6,000 travelling Toffees behind the goal held their breath as Leighton Baines stepped forward and curled an unbelievable shot into the top corner of the net! The tie went to penalties and after Anelka and Cole missed for Chelsea it was

down to Phil Neville to stroke home the winning kick. What a day!

7 BLUES CALL THE TOON!
5 March

After the huge disappointment of losing at home to Reading in the FA Cup, Everton had four days to re-group and get back on track. They did it superbly well at Newcastle with an excellent performance that earned a much-needed win. The Toon actually scored first through Leon Best but in-form Leon Osman equalised in the

31st minute and then four minutes later Phil Jagielka turned home what proved to be the winner.

Continued on **P10**

TOP TEN FROM TEN-ELEVEN

Continued from **P9**

8 HUNGRY BLUES TAME THE WOLVES!

9 April

Everton didn't just win at Wolves in April, they did it in fabulous style with three terrific first-half goals. First of all, Jermaine Beckford made a brilliant run to glance home a perfect cross from Leon Osman in the 21st minute, and then the skipper took over! Phil Neville had waited a long time for a Premier League goal but when it came at Molineux it was a cracker – an angled drive from the edge of the box. Just before half-time though, we got the goal of the game. Diniyar Bilyaletdinov collected the ball on the half-way line and carried it forward before unleashing a ferocious shot that flew into the top corner of the net.

9 CITY GET DONE AGAIN!

7 May

Manchester City must be sick of the sight of Everton! Even when Yaya Toure gave

them a half-time lead at Goodison, they couldn't hold on to take anything from the game. A magnificent second-half display from Everton was rewarded with a towering header from

Sylvain Distin to make the score all-square and then a tremendously brave header from Leon Osman for a 72nd minute winner.

10 BECKS BEATS THE BLUES!

22 May

Jermaine Beckford enjoyed a fine first season in the Premier League but in true fashion he certainly left the best until last! The Toffees had 10 men following the dismissal of Seamus Coleman but on 74 minutes Beckford got the ball on the edge of his own box and started running with it. He just kept going, taking on half a dozen Chelsea players before placing a composed finish past Petr Cech to send Goodison wild! What a way to end the season!

END OF SEASON AWARDS

The 6th Annual Everton End of Season Awards evening was held in May 2011 at the BT Convention Centre on the world-famous Liverpool waterfront and was hosted by Ray Stubbs.

As usual, the Chairman, the Board of Directors, the manager and the entire first-team squad were all in attendance and it was another splendid Everton evening.

The star of the show was England defender Leighton Baines, who scooped THREE major prizes! Seamus Coleman was only one behind him and Leon Osman joined David Moyes in winning the Chairman's Blue Blood award. Duncan Ferguson received a hero's welcome when he stepped forward to accept his Everton Giant award and the Academy title-winning Under-18s were also acknowledged on the night.

SEAMUS COLEMAN

The young Irishman was plying his trade for League of Ireland team, Sligo Rovers, when he was picked up by Everton in January 2009 for a bargain fee of £60,000.

It was a massive step for the quiet boy from the village of Killybegs but Seamus adapted to his new environment so well that he was short-listed for the 2010/11 PFA Young Player of the Year.

It represented an astonishing rise for him but he recalls the time that his Everton career was very nearly over before it had begun.

"Yes, it was a worrying time for me when I picked up an infection in my foot during the summer tour of America in 2009," he said. "I couldn't go outside the hotel for virtually the whole trip and it was a bit of a nightmare to be honest."

Thankfully he made a full recovery and was soon running out at the world-famous Stadium of Light, home of the mighty Benfica, for his Everton first-team debut! The Blues lost the match 5-0 but it's a night that Seamus will never forget.

"It was a very disappointing result but I had to pinch myself before the game to make sure I wasn't dreaming!" he said. "To be lining up for a Europa League match against a team as famous as Benfica was unbelievable. It was a proud night for me."

His Premier League debut wasn't long after and Seamus made a terrific contribution when he came on as a substitute against Tottenham Hotspur. Everton were trailing 2-0 but Seamus came off the bench to help turn things around with a sparkling display that eventually earned a 2-2 draw.

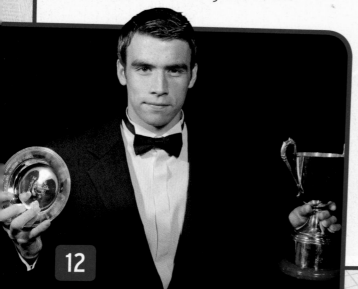

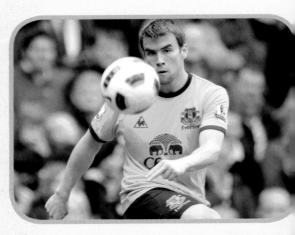

"I got a lot of praise after that game but I was just happy to have made a contribution," he said modestly.

The supporters were rather more enthusiastic about his cameo role that saw him run the Tottenham defence ragged!

A star was born but it took a loan spell away at Blackpool for Seamus to really start to flourish. He played a big part in helping Blackpool to promotion to the Premier League in 2009/10. He looks back at his time with Ian Holloway with real affection.

"It was a great experience for me," he said. "Ian Holloway has a reputation as being a bit mad but he was brilliant with me. I learned a lot at Blackpool and it really helped me when I came back to Everton."

There was never any chance of Blackpool ever making the move permanent and so Seamus came back to Goodison for the 2010/11 campaign and had a great season, scoring six goals and really catching the eye.

"I really felt like a part of it last season," he said. "It's a great dressing-room to be in. The lads are great and there are plenty of players I can turn to for advice if I need any. I've come a long way since Sligo Rovers but I'll always be grateful for the start they gave me. But I'm an Everton player now and there's nowhere I'd rather be!"

13

PLAYER PROFILES

TIM HOWARD

Date of Birth: 06/03/1979 in New Jersey, USA

Previous Clubs: New York Metro Stars, Manchester United

Everton debut: v Watford (home) August 2006

Stats: 226 appearances, 0 goals

Fact: Tim was the first American player to win the FA Cup in 2004

What's the Answer? How many penalties did Tim save in the 2009 FA Cup semi-final?

2011/12   Appearances: Goals: What's the answer?

TONY HIBBERT

Date of Birth: 20/02/1981 in Liverpool, England

Previous Clubs: None

Everton debut: v West Ham United (away) March 2001

Stats: 273 appearances, 0 goals

Fact: Tony was tripped up by Stuart Pearce and won a penalty for Everton on his debut in 2001

What's the Answer? What competition did Tony win with Everton in 1998?

2011/12   Appearances: Goals: What's the answer?

Answers on **page 61**

LEIGHTON BAINES

Date of Birth: 11/12/1984 in Liverpool, England

Previous Clubs: Wigan Athletic

Everton debut: v Blackburn Rovers (home) August 2007

Stats: 160 appearances, 10 goals

Fact: Leighton played for Wigan in the 2006 League Cup final against Manchester United

What's the Answer? Did Leighton score or miss in the 2011 FA Cup penalty shoot-out at Chelsea?

2011/12	Appearances:	Goals:	What's the answer?

SYLVAIN DISTIN

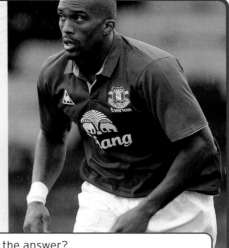

Date of Birth: 16/12/1977 in Bagnolet, France

Previous Clubs: Gueugnon, Paris St Germain, Newcastle United, Manchester City, Portsmouth

Everton debut: v Wigan Athletic, August 2009

Stats: 82 appearances, 4 goals

Fact: Sylvain won the FA Cup with Portsmouth in 2008

What's the Answer? Sylvain scored his first Everton goal in the UEFA Cup against which Greek team?

2011/12	Appearances:	Goals:	What's the answer?

PHIL JAGIELKA

Date of Birth: 17/08/1982 in Sale, England

Previous Clubs: Sheffield United

Everton debut: v Tottenham Hotspur (away) August 2007

Stats: 141 appearances, 4 goals

Fact: Phil's older brother Steve was a professional footballer with Stoke City and Shrewsbury

What's the Answer? What is the nickname of Phil's previous club, Sheffield United?

2011/12	Appearances:	Goals:	What's the answer?

JOHNNY HEITINGA

Date of Birth: 15/11/1983 in Alphen aan den Rijn, Holland

Previous Clubs: Ajax, Athletico Madrid

Everton debut: v Fulham (away) September 2009

Stats: 66 appearances, 1 goal

Fact: In 2010, Johnny became the 5th player to be sent off in a World Cup final

What's the Answer? Which country did John's Holland beat in the 2010 World Cup semi-final?

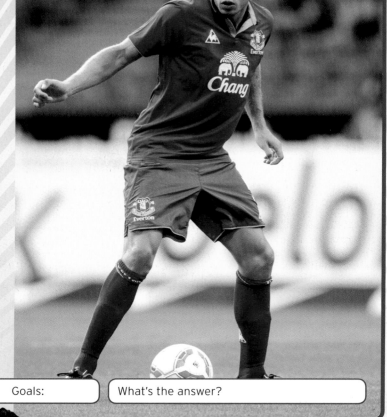

2011/12	Appearances:	Goals:	What's the answer?

DINIYAR BILYALETDINOV

Date of Birth: 27/02/1985 in Moscow, Russia

Previous Clubs: Lokomotiv Moscow

Everton debut: v Wigan Athletic (home) August 2009

Stats: 65 appearances, 9 goals

Fact: His full name is worth 33 points in Scrabble!

What's the Answer? Against which team did Diniyar score his Everton Goal of the Season in 2009/10?

2011/12	Appearances:	Goals:	What's the answer?

LEON OSMAN

Date of Birth: 17/05/1981 in Billinge, England

Previous Clubs: None

Everton debut: v Tottenham Hotspur (away) Jan 2003

Stats: 269 appearances, 38 goals

Fact: Before playing for Everton's first team, Leon had loan spells at Carlisle United and Derby County

What's the Answer? When Everton reached the FA Cup final in 2009, Leon scored the 3rd Round winner against which League Two team?

2011/12	Appearances:	Goals:	What's the answer?

SEAMUS COLEMAN

Date of Birth: 11/10/1988 in Donegal, Republic of Ireland

Previous Clubs: Sligo Rovers

Everton debut: v Benfica (away) October 2009

Stats: 47 appearances, 6 goals

Fact: Seamus was born in the Donegal fishing village of Killybegs

What's the Answer? In 2010, Seamus appeared in a play-off final at Wembley for which team?

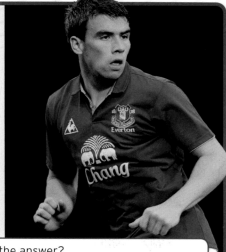

2011/12	Appearances:	Goals:	What's the answer?

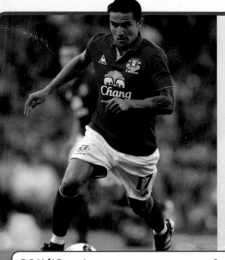

TIM CAHILL

Date of Birth: 06/12/1979 in Sydney, Australia

Previous Clubs: Millwall

Everton debut: v Manchester United (away) August 2004

Stats: 237 appearances, 65 goals

Fact: In 2006, Tim became the first ever Australian player to score in a World Cup finals match.

What's the Answer? Tim has played in two FA Cup finals. True or false?

2011/12	Appearances:	Goals:	What's the answer?

JACK RODWELL

Date of Birth: 11/03/1991 in Birkdale, England

Previous Clubs: None

Everton debut: v AZ Alkmaar (away) December 2007

Stats: 92 appearances, 6 goals

Fact: Jack's uncle Tony played over 150 games for Blackpool in the 1990s

What's the Answer? Jack's first two goals in Europe came in a 4-0 win against which team at Goodison Park in 2009?

2011/12	Appearances:	Goals:	What's the answer?

MAROUANE FELLAINI

Date of Birth: 22/11/1987 in Eterbeek, Belgium

Previous Clubs: Standard Liege

Everton debut: v Stoke City (away) September 2008

Stats: 94 appearances, 15 goals

Fact: Marouane played for Belgium at the Olympic Games in 2008

What's the Answer? For which other country did Marouane have the option of playing before he chose Belgium?

2011/12	Appearances:	Goals:	What's the answer?

PHIL NEVILLE

Date of Birth: 21/02/1977 in Bury, England

Previous Clubs: Manchester United

Everton debut: Villarreal (home) August 2005

Stats: 242 appearances, 4 goals

Fact: Phil was just 19 years old when he made his England debut against China in 1996.

What's the Answer? Phil's only goal of last season came against which team?

2011/12	Appearances:	Goals:	What's the answer?

Answers on **page 61**

LOUIS SAHA

Date of Birth: 08/08/1978 in Paris, France

Previous Clubs: Metz, Newcastle United, Fulham, Manchester United

Everton debut: v Hull City (away) September 2008

Stats: 95 appearances, 33 goals

Fact: Louis scored the fastest ever FA Cup final goal when he found the net after just 25 seconds against Chelsea at Wembley in 2009.

What's the Answer? When Louis scored four against Blackpool at Goodison last season, who scored the other goal in a 5-3 win?

2011/12	Appearances:	Goals:	What's the answer?

VICTOR ANICHEBE

Date of Birth: 23/04/1988 in Anambra, Nigeria

Previous Clubs: None

Everton debut: v Chelsea (home FA Cup) January 2006

Stats: 119 appearances, 12 goals

Fact: Victor played for Nigeria in 2008 Olympic Games and won a silver medal

What's the Answer? In 2007/08, Victor scored four goals for Everton in which competition?

2011/12	Appearances:	Goals:	What's the answer?

JUNIOR QUIZ

Take time out from enjoying your 2012 Everton Annual and test your knowledge of your favourite club.

See how many of these 20 questions you get right and then compare your score with your friends.

18-20 You're a Premier League winner
15-17 You've qualified for the Champions League
10-14 A comfortable mid-table finish
6-9 A disappointing lower-half position
0-5 Oh dear, relegation looms for you!

1. What is the name of the Irish team that Everton signed Seamus Coleman from?

2. For which country does Diniyar Bilyaletdinov play?

3. History – in what year did Everton last win the FA Cup?

4. Which team knocked Everton out of last season's Carling Cup?

5. David Moyes played for Celtic or Rangers when he was a youngster?

6. Is Phil Neville older or younger than his brother, Gary?

7. Who scored Everton's goals in the 2-2 draw at Liverpool last season?

8. Last season, Everton recorded 5-1 victories against which two Football League teams?

9. For what team did Jermaine Beckford play before he joined Everton?

10. History – who is the only man to have scored more Everton goals than Graeme Sharp?

11. Who was the Everton manager before David Moyes?

12. For which team, other than Everton, has Tim Cahill played in an FA Cup final?

13. In which country was Sylvain Distin born?

14. History – how many times have Everton won the FA Cup – 4, 5 or 6?

15. Which two USA teams did Everton play in the summer of 2011?

16. For which international team does Victor Anichebe play?

17. Who joined Everton from a team called Standard Liege?

18. History – in which year did Everton last win the League title?

19. Who was sent off against West Brom during our last away game of last season?

20. What has Tim Howard got in common with Fulham's Clint Dempsey and Bolton's Stuart Holden?

Answers on **page 61**

FELLI IN BANGKOK

During the 2010/11 season, Everton Football Club announced an extension to their sponsorship deal with Chang Beer.

As part of the celebrations, midfield star Marouane Fellaini jetted out to the Thailand capital, Bangkok, to meet employees at the media launch of the new deal.

The big Belgian was mobbed wherever he went in Bangkok and he was delighted to have the opportunity to meet up not only with Chang staff and dignitaries but with the many Everton supporters to have been recruited in Thailand since the sponsorship arrangement started in 2004.

See if you can name the Premier League teams who are sponsored by these companies...

1 AON

2 Fly Emirates

3 Samsung

4 Etihad Airways

5 Northern Rock

Answers on **page 61**

EVERTONFC.COM

evertonfc.com is the Club's official website and prides itself on being the best, easiest to use and most innovative in the Premier League.

Everything Everton does on the site is with fans in mind...have you checked out these great features?

EvertonLive: All the Everton news and fan comments from Twitter, Facebook, the BlueRoom and, of course, evertonfc.com in one central place.

JERMAINE BECKFORD CHECKS THE LATEST NEWS ON EVERTONFC.COM!

evertontv: All video-on-demand content is now free to registered users of the site, meaning you can hear direct from your favourite players – as well as checking out the latest action.

MatchDay: A live ticker of news from around the grounds, live commentary and a new match centre boasting more statistics, pictures and chances for you to have your say.

Personalised Homepage: The opportunity to select the content that interests you on the main page of the site.

ePredictor: Take on the popular match prediction game – now with the opportunity to pit yourself against your Evertonian friends.

Your Greatest XI: Dixie, Ball, Sharp, Big Duncan – who makes your best-ever Everton XI? Choose here and share your selection with your friends.

The BlueRoom: The Club's online Forum is easy to use and links up closely with the main website.

OTHER PLACES TO CHECK OUT

As well as **evertonfc.com** you can get your Everton fix from Facebook and Twitter, where thousands of other Evertonians head to find out the latest news and chat about what's going on at the Club.

Visit us on Facebook at **facebook.com/everton** or Twitter at **twitter.com/youreverton** to get the very latest!

evertonfc.com is the first port of call for all True Blues!

EVERTON TV

evertontv, Everton's FREE online video channel, follows the Blues wherever they go and gets great access to the players to do interviews.

Check out our photos of **evertontv** in action.

Here's **evertontv** catching up with Leighton Baines earlier this year. Bainesy has grown into one of Everton's most popular players since arriving in 2007 and won the Player of the Season award for last season. Although he's a little shy at times, he doesn't mind chatting to **evertontv** and is one of the best players to interview.

This is Everton legend Graeme Sharp and current favourite Leon Osman providing live **evertontv** commentary during the Summer tour of the USA. We provide audio commentary from every match during the Premier League season and we often provide video coverage of the friendlies. On this occasion Ossie wasn't fit to play so he joined Sharpy to provide expert analysis and interact with viewers.

evertontv enjoys VIP access to all sorts of events and one of the most glamorous is the End of Season Awards Evening. **evertontv** interviews all the winners as they come off stage – which meant on this occasion that an extremely rare interview with newly-crowned Everton giant Duncan Ferguson was recorded!

ACADEMY CHAMPIONS

Everton Under-18s ended the 2010/11 season as the national champions!

Under the guidance of coaches Neil Dewsnip and Kevin Sheedy, the Toffees first secured the area title, then defeated Aston Villa in the national semi-final before beating Fulham in the final to take the crown.

It capped a remarkably consistent season for Everton, who lost only five fixtures throughout the campaign. The boys thrashed Liverpool 4-0, did the double over a highly-rated Manchester United and went on a terrific twelve-game unbeaten run from early February to the end of April that went a long way towards securing the regional title.

Even so, it was nerve-jangling stuff. After a last game defeat at Leeds, Everton needed Wolverhampton Wanderers to get a result away to Liverpool to prevent the Reds from stealing the title.

"Players and staff all gathered around a big screen at Finch Farm and we watched the Liverpool v Wolves game on LFC tv," explained Dewsnip. "There was tremendous excitement when Wolves went 2-1 up but it was terrible when Liverpool equalised late on. Another Liverpool goal would have cost us the league."

> "EVERYONE CONTRIBUTED S[O]
> EVERYBODY DESERVES IT.
> THE WHOLE CLUB SHOULD B[E]
> VERY PROUD OF THESE BOYS[."]
> Kevin Sheedy

CAPTAIN JAKE BIDWELL WITH THE TROPHY

Thankfully, Wolves held on for a point and Everton were home and dry. The next hurdle was a week later at Finch Farm when Aston Villa came for the national semi-final. The Blues had to come from behind before finally clinching a 3-2 win thanks to a fabulous long-range goal from Conor McAleny.

As for the final, the omens were not the best for Everton. Fulham won the toss to have the game played at Craven Cottage and the date of the game was Friday 13th!

With nine minutes to go, Fulham were leading 1-0 and it seemed as though national runners-up would be as good as it got for Everton. But the spirited and highly talented young men in royal blue jerseys had other ideas.

In the 81st minute, the home side failed to clear a free kick and Adam Thomas took advantage to equalise and then with just four minutes to go, substitute George Waring headed the winning goal for Everton!

It sealed an incredible achievement. Everton's Academy has a fantastic reputation for producing players and now they could legitimately call themselves 'the best Under-18s team in the country'.

GEORGE WARING SCORES THE WINNER

WELCOME TO FINCH FARM

The magnificent Everton Football Club training complex at Finch Farm is where the players go through their paces in the build-up to all the big games.

It's where David Moyes and his coaching staff prepare the lads for the rigours of the Premier League.

But Finch Farm is much more than just a venue for the players to get fit and sharp enough to play top-flight football...

• It is also a place for legends to pop in! Here we see England's 1966 World Cup winning goalkeeper Gordon Banks pictured with Everton's current stopper, Tim Howard.

• It is also a place for the players to train with the Academy. Every now and then, the first-team players pop over to the Academy side of Finch Farm for a kickabout with the youngsters.

• It is also a place for David Moyes and the players to speak to the press - here is the manager having a laugh and a joke with Sylvain Distin during a press conference in the Finch Farm Media Theatre.

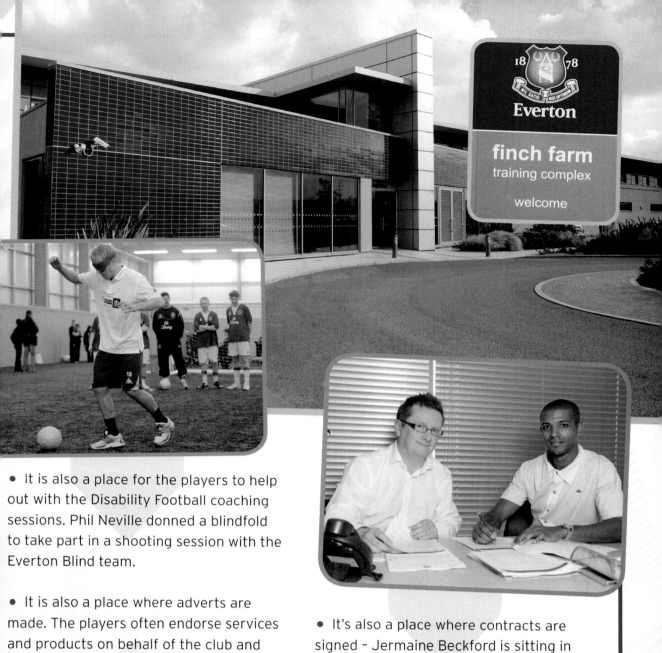

- It is also a place for the players to help out with the Disability Football coaching sessions. Phil Neville donned a blindfold to take part in a shooting session with the Everton Blind team.

- It is also a place where adverts are made. The players often endorse services and products on behalf of the club and here Jack Rodwell is posing next to a very expensive brand new car (and, no, he didn't get to keep it!!)

- It's also a place where contracts are signed - Jermaine Beckford is sitting in the Club Secretary's Finch Farm office waiting to sign his.

TEN-YEAR TONY!

Tony Hibbert made his Everton debut as long ago as March 2001.

He was called up by the then manager Walter Smith to play for the first team against West Ham United at Upton Park and there wasn't even time for his dad to get to the game!

"It was a bit of a surprise to say the least and my dad was gutted because he was in Liverpool when I told him and there was no way he could have got to Upton Park in time," he said.

"But he listened to every kick on the radio and he's been to most of my games since then!"

"I HAD GOOD SENIOR PROFESSIONALS AROUND ME WHEN I BROKE INTO THE TEAM SO HOPEFULLY THE YOUNG LADS WE'VE GOT NOW WILL CONSIDER ME TO BE SIMILAR."

Tony's debut went well. An Everton team that included Duncan Ferguson, Thomas Gravesen and Michael Ball won 2-0 at West Ham and young Tony earned the first goal when he was tripped inside the box for a penalty!

"It was just before half-time and Stuart Pearce brought me down for a penalty," he recalled. "David Unsworth scored it and we went on from there to win the game. I don't think I've been in the penalty box since!"

These days, of course, Tony is an elder statesman of the Everton squad and, as such, he always tries to keep an eye on the young players who come into the team.

"I do because I know what it's like to be a local boy having come through the Academy to play for the first team," he said.

"I had good senior professionals around me when I broke into the team so hopefully the young lads we've got now will consider me to be similar. I'm not one for shouting and screaming in the dressing room but I'm always there if one of the young boys needs any advice."

During his ten years in the first team picture, Tony had the distinction of creating a new record when he became the player with the most European appearances for the club. When he captained the team against BATE Borisov at Goodison Park in 2009 it was his 20th appearance in Europe for Everton and it took him one clear of men like Brian Labone and Colin Harvey.

"That was a great honour for me," he admitted. "To be honest, I didn't even know that I was anywhere near the record until somebody told me and I was made up about it. To be at the top of any list at this great football club is something special and I just hope there are more European appearances to come."

EVERTON IN THE USA

David Moyes took his players across the Atlantic Ocean in the summer of 2011 for a pre-season trip that included matches against MLS outfits Philadelphia Union and DC United.

The east coast of the USA was in the middle of a heat-wave when the Everton party jetted in and the temperatures regularly topped 100 degrees Fahrenheit!

As well as the games, there was much to do for the Everton party...

There were pre-match press conferences at both the PPL Park Stadium, Philadelphia and the RFK Stadium in the capital city.

There is huge interest in Premier League football in the States and both events were well attended by American media.

The boss was joined by Mikel Arteta and Phil Neville in Philadelphia and by Phil Jagielka in Washington.

(The only question the manager didn't answer was from an American reporter who wanted to know about the phone-tapping scandal that was going on in the UK at the time!)

HEITINGA AGAINST UNION

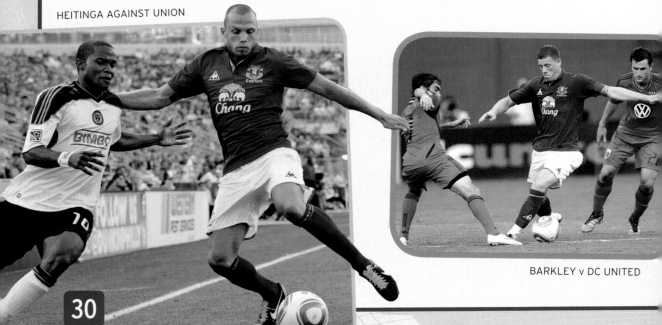

BARKLEY v DC UNITED

30

The players also went out and about to meet the fans. Leighton Baines, Phil Jagielka and Tim Cahill met some ex-pat Evertonians in Philly, and Phil Neville, Leon Osman and Seamus Coleman did likewise later in the week in Washington.

As well as US-based Toffees, there was the usual gang of Evertonians who had travelled over to watch the games, and they were all rewarded with a couple of open training sessions.

David Moyes, Steve Round and the rest of the coaching staff put the players through their paces in front of some very appreciative spectators at both venues.

For the record, Everton lost one and won one of their two matches.

BLUES MEET THE FANS AND FACE THE PRESS

They went down to an 87th-minute goal to Philadelphia Union but bounced back to defeat DC United 3-1, thanks to goals from Victor Anichebe, Diniyar Bilyaletdinov and Magaye Gueye.

The USA is a popular venue for English teams during pre-season and Everton certainly enjoyed their stay last summer.

TON AND DC UNITED

CONTINENTAL

Some of the most popular players to have worn the royal blue jersey of Everton in the last 20 years have come from countries all over the world.

In the team of 2011/12 the likes of Mikel Arteta, Tim Howard, Marouane Fellaini and Tim Cahill are idolised by the supporters.

Here's a selection of the most popular continental players to have played for The Toffees since the Premier League started back in 1992...

ANDREI KANCHELSKIS
60 appearances, 22 goals

Kanchelskis was a speedy international winger for **RUSSIA** who made his name in English football with Manchester United. He signed for Everton in 1995 and scored 16 goals in his first season.

JOE-MAX MOORE
64 appearances, 10 goals

Moore was born in Oklahoma and played 100 times for the **USA**. He was a star name in the American MLS League with New England Revolution when Everton signed him in 1999.

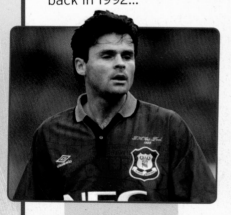

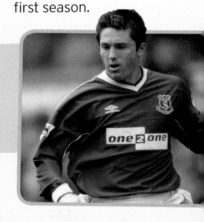

ANDERS LIMPAR
82 appearances, 6 goals

Limpar was signed by Everton from Arsenal in 1994 and was a key member of the team that won the FA Cup final at Wembley in 1995. He was a **SWEDISH** international who played in the 1990 and 1994 World Cups.

DANIEL AMOKACHI
54 appearances, 14 goals

Amokachi played in the 1994 and 1998 World Cup finals for **NIGERIA** and he signed for Everton from Belgian club Bruges in the summer of 1994. He famously scored two goals for the Blues in the 1995 FA Cup semi-final.

TOMASZ RADZINSKI

101 appearances, 26 goals

Radzinski was one of the quickest forwards to play in the Premier League. Despite being born in **POLAND** he represented **CANADA** at international level and scored his first goal for them against Brazil!

And anyone remember this guy...?

OLIVIER DACOURT

36 appearances, 3 goals

Dacourt only had one season at Everton (1998/99) but he played well and scored against Liverpool! After leaving Everton he had spells with Leeds United, Roma, Inter Milan and Fulham. He played for **FRANCE** in the 2004 Euros.

DAVID GINOLA

7 appearances, 0 goals

FRENCH-born Ginola was one of the most famous international players to have played for the club. He wasn't with Everton long, though, and never reached the heights he had at Newcastle and Tottenham Hotspur.

THOMAS GRAVESEN

168 appearances, 12 goals

One of the most popular foreign players ever to play for the club, **DANISH** international Gravesen had two spells at Everton, playing for Real Madrid and Celtic in between.

LI TIE

40 appearances, 0 goals

Li Tie was a **CHINESE** international who only joined Everton in 2002 as part of a sponsorship deal but then played regularly in the first team. A very popular figure at Goodison, he made his Premier League debut on the same day as Wayne Rooney!

WORDSEARCH

E	C	G	S	E	I	V	A	D	N	K	H
I	N	R	R	L	C	F	K	O	M	T	G
T	O	A	T	Z	R	A	S	A	I	T	R
T	S	V	G	L	J	N	R	M	W	T	I
A	T	E	M	N	H	T	S	S	F	G	E
E	A	S	H	O	Y	Y	W	H	L	L	W
B	W	E	J	N	A	P	T	Z	J	E	W
T	M	N	K	N	Y	E	N	O	O	R	Y
V	J	N	P	I	S	T	O	N	E	J	R
K	I	L	B	A	N	E	N	M	D	Z	D
W	R	I	G	H	T	N	W	E	M	T	V
F	E	R	G	U	S	O	N	R	B	Z	B

Inside this grid we've hidden the names of 15 players who have played for Everton while David Moyes has been the manager. See how many you can find... Remember the words can go horizontally, vertically and diagonally in all eight directions.

BEATTIE	GRAVESEN	PISTONE
BENT	JOHNSON	ROONEY
CARSLEY	KILBANE	WATSON
DAVIES	MARTYN	WEIR
FERGUSON	NAYSMITH	WRIGHT

Answers on **page 61**

EVERTON IN THE COMMUNITY

Football is not the only thing that goes on at Everton Football Club! The Club's staff and players have been busy off the pitch too, helping lots of people in the local community.

From opening new sports clubs to painting hospitals to playing ping-pong (!), the players and the Blues' official charity, Everton in the Community, have been working hard to improve the lives of disadvantaged children and adults on Merseyside.

Everton in the Community runs a range of schemes to teach people about health, education and accepting others who may be different to you. Here's a taste of what we have been up to this year...

▶ Mikel Arteta visited Alder Hey Children's Hospital to help decorate a new restaurant for parents to use while their children receive treatment. Mikel helped volunteers paint the walls blue (of course!) and made sure everything was just right.

▶ Sylvain Distin helped launch a new badminton club as part of the Premier League for Sport initiative to help more young people progress in Olympic sports. The Frenchman even joined in the fun, playing a few games against British No. 3 Harry Wright!

▶ John Heitinga demonstrated his ping pong skills when he visited a new local table tennis club. John surprised everyone by how good he was, and said he had been practising with Arsenal's Robin van Persie in a tournament at the Dutch World Cup training base in South Africa!

If you want to get involved in one of Everton in the Community's clubs or find out ways in which you can help raise money to help people who may not be as lucky as yourself, visit evertonfc.com/community.

ACADEMY DAY

One of the most eagerly anticipated days of the year at the Finch Farm training complex is the day that David Moyes and his first-team squad finish training early and pop across to join in with the young boys of the Everton Academy.

It's the day when you get an eight-year-old centre-forward trying to push the ball through the legs of Phil Jagielka! Or you see the bizarre sight of a 10-year-old goalkeeper trying to narrow his angles as Jermaine Beckford runs through on goal!

Or what about Leon Osman playfully fouling as many youngsters as he can in a desperate attempt to help his team to win! It's a terrific day for everyone concerned and the senior professionals enjoy it every bit as much as the boys.

"It's great fun and we all look forward to it," said Leon Osman. "The kids obviously relish the chance to have a game of football with us and if any of the senior players get 'nut-megged' they get stick for weeks!"

ACADEMY AWARDS

2010/11 was a very successful season for the Everton Academy... and this was reflected in the prestigious Awards Evening that was staged at the impressive St George's Hall, in the heart of Liverpool.

Tim Cahill and Jack Rodwell called in to present some of the awards as the Academy Players of the Year for all the age groups from Under-7s through to Under-18s were honoured.

There were also awards for the Academy Goal of the Season and for the young teams who had won tournaments abroad.

In May 2010, the boys born in 1999 won The Sendin Cup in Epinay, France and the boys born in 1997 won the C.V.V Zwervers Competition in Capelle aan den IJssel in Holland.

Then in July 2010 the boys born in 2000 and 2001 won the The BWCI Mini Soccer Festival in Guernsey.

Here's a picture from a previous tournament abroad that Everton Under-12s competed in. You might not recognise the captain or the goalkeeper but do you know who the third player is trotting out onto the pitch?

Yes, that's right – it's Wayne Rooney about to star for Everton in Geneva!

Wayne came right through the ranks at Everton before making his Premier League debut at the age of 16.

A HERO FOR CLUB & COUNTRY

Tim Howard was born in New Jersey, USA, and when he graduated from North Brunswick Township High School he excelled at both basketball and soccer and he had a decision to make.

Thankfully for future fans of the USA national team, he elected to put all his efforts into soccer! Originally a midfield player, he soon discovered that his future may be further back on the field...

"I loved playing basketball and I still do when I get the chance," he said. "But I preferred soccer and played for the USA at both Under-15 and Under-17. It's true that I was an outfield player for a while but my future was always going to be in goal."

Tim played for the USA at the 1999 World Youth Championships in Nigeria and then he was back-up to Brad Friedel at the 2000 Olympic Games in Sydney.

His first full cap duly arrived in 2002 when USA played Ecuador.

"That was an incredible moment for me and my family," said Tim. "To represent your country at any level at any sport is a wonderful thing to do and I saw my first cap as a reward for all the hard work that I had put in over the years and for all the help and support I had from my family. It was tough at that time because as well as Brad, we also had Kasey Keller available, so it wasn't as though the USA was short of goalkeepers!"

These days, of course, Tim is the undisputed USA Number 1 and he has appeared for his country in World Cup, Gold Cup and Confederation Cup competitions.

However, playing for your country when your club side is about 3,000 miles away poses problems!

"Yes, it does!" he smiled. "There can be a lot of travelling during the season but if you prepare yourself properly then it doesn't become an issue.

"I always make sure I get some sleep on the trans-Atlantic flights and the manager, David Moyes, is great with regards to my rest and recovery. He knows that I will have trained properly with the national team and that I will always be 100% ready for the next Everton game.

"I'm not alone either because a lot of the players play for their country. Tim Cahill, for example, has to fly half way around the world for an international home match!"

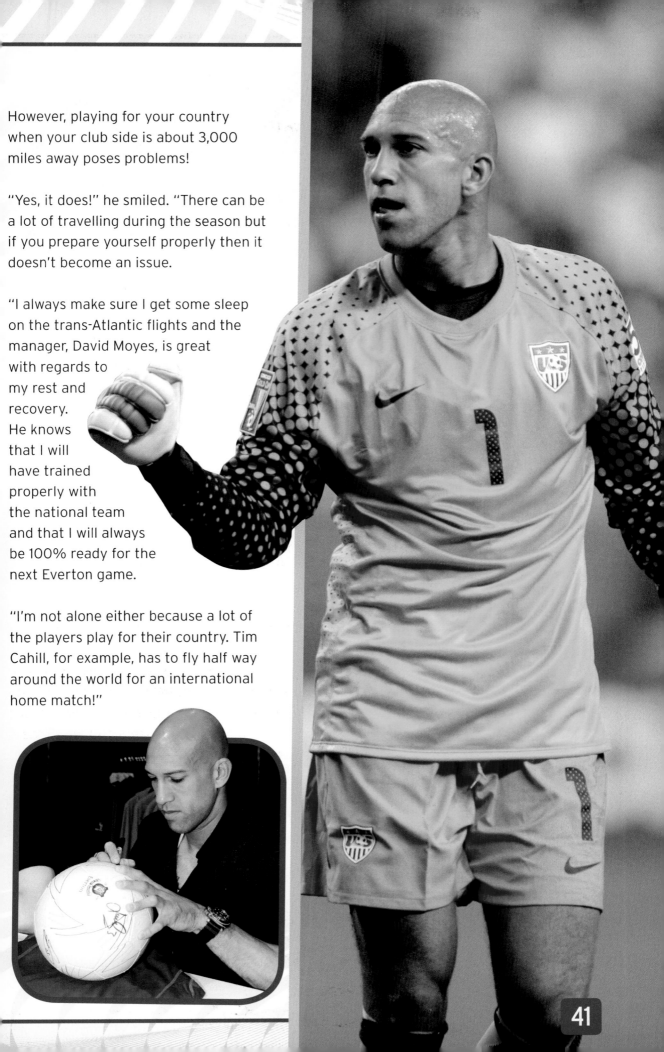

HAT-TRICK HEROES

Only one player scored a hat-trick for Everton last season – can you remember who it was?

That's right, Louis Saha against Blackpool on a very wet and windy afternoon at Goodison Park. In fact, Saha went one better and scored FOUR goals in the match, becoming the first player to score that many at Goodison Park since Joe Royle in 1971!

Here are some more Everton players who have scored hat-tricks down the years...we've left the opposition blank so you can try and guess who they scored them against by the clues...

Answers on **page 61**

HAT-TRICK HERO **YAKABU**

In February 2008, Everton defeated a team from Denmark in the UEFA Cup. After a fine 2-0 win in the first leg, the Toffees wrapped it all up in the second leg thanks to a tremendous 6-1 victory at Goodison. The hero of the night was YAKUBU, who scored a hat-trick to put the team from Bergen out of the competition.

OPPONENT

HAT-TRICK HERO **STEVE WATSON**

In September 2003 Everton thrashed a team from Yorkshire at Goodison Park. STEVE WATSON scored a hat-trick in the 4-0 win, with Duncan Ferguson scoring the other goal. England goalkeeper Paul Robinson was between the sticks for the opposition.

OPPONENT

HAT-TRICK HERO KEVIN CAMPBELL

Everton's last home fixture of the 1998/99 season was against a London team. It was a very one-sided match with Everton winning 6-0! KEVIN CAMPBELL scored a hat-trick against a team that included Rio Ferdinand and Frank Lampard.

OPPONENT

HAT-TRICK HERO DUNCAN FERGUSON

DUNCAN FERGUSON only ever scored one hat-trick for Everton and it came in December 1997 against a team from Lancashire who played in white shirts. Ferguson scored twice in the first half and once in the second against the team who had moved into their new stadium at the start of that season.

OPPONENT

HAT-TRICK HERO GRAEME SHARP

Everton's FA Cup tie with the Owls in 1988 went to THREE replays before it was decided. Then, amazingly, after three draws Everton won 5-0 at the famous home of their opponents - with GRAEME SHARP scoring three times. And guess what? The half-time score was 5-0!

OPPONENT

HAT-TRICK HERO GARY LINEKER

BBC Match of the Day presenter GARY LINEKER played one season for Everton (1985/86) but he scored THREE hat-tricks! The first one came at the end of August in a 4-1 win against a team from the Midlands that was relegated from the Premier League last season.

OPPONENT

43

EVERTON SONGS

"WE SHALL NOT BE MOVED"

We shall not, We shall not be moved // We shall not, We shall not be moved // Just like the team that's gonna win the FA Cup // We shall not be moved!

"TELL ME MA!"

Tell Me Ma, Me Ma // I don't want no tea, no tea I going to Wem-ber-ley // Tell Me Ma, Me Ma

"IF YER KNOW YOUR HISTORY"

It's a grand old team to play for // And it's a grand old team to support // And if you know your history // It's enough to make your heart go whoah-oh-oh-oh // We don't care what the red side says // What the heck do we care // Because we only know // That if there's gonna be a show // Then the Everton boys will be there.

EVERTON MEET THE FA

In January 2009, Everton began a series of visits to officially affiliated Supporters' Clubs and by the end of last season, club officials and players (past and present) had been to places as far away as Australia, Wales, Dublin, Belfast and London – as well as lots more a bit closer to home! The aim of the visits is to meet with the members, inform them of any relevant and important developments at the Club, and to listen to what the fans have got to say.

MAROUANE FELLAINI ENTERTAINING THE FANS

Each evening has been really enjoyable and the feedback from the supporters has been brilliant. The undoubted highlight of each visit is the opportunity for the Everton supporters to meet the players and get some autographs and photographs with their heroes – as well as getting the wonderful opportunity to ask them a few questions!

The players themselves have also enjoyed getting out and about and meeting the loyal fans who form the many Everton Supporters' Clubs around the UK and beyond.

Leon Osman joined club officials in Chorley, Lancashire.

OSSIE POPPED IN TO SEE THE CHORLEY BLUES

"IT WAS A REALLY GOOD NIGHT. I'D INJURED MY FOOT IN THE PREVIOUS GAME SO I DIDN'T REALLY FEEL LIKE GOING OUT BUT I'M GLAD I DID. IT WAS GREAT TO MEET THE CHORLEY GANG AND WE HAD A GOOD LAUGH!"
Leon Osman

"It was a really good night," he said. "I'd injured my foot in the previous game so I didn't really feel like going out but I'm glad I did. It was great to meet the Chorley gang and we had a good laugh!"

Supporters' Clubs closer to Goodison have also enjoyed official visits. Mikel Arteta popped into the Taxi Club on Walton Lane and Marouane Fellaini met the Everton (Goodison) Supporters in the famous Winslow Pub just over the road from the stadium.
In fact, during that night, Felli was proposed to by an over enthusiastic female Toffee in the audience!

He reluctantly declined the offer!

These visits are usually also attended by the club's CEO Robert Elstone, legend Graeme Sharp and various other Everton officials. They are terrific Everton nights but you have to be a member of an affiliated Supporters' Club to be able to enjoy them.

For details of how to do this, simply follow the link below.

evertonfc.com/club/supporters-groups

EVERTON INTERNATIONALS

The Everton training ground at Finch Farm is always a quiet place to be during the international breaks because so many of the players are away representing their country.

David Moyes holds his breath while the lads are in action as he waits for them to report back for club duty in one piece!

Here are some of your favourite Everton stars playing for their countries. See how many of the countries you can name...

Answers on **page 61**

Diniyar Bilyaletdinov challenges for the ball with Yousef Ahmed during the

[   ] versus

[   ] friendly in

March 2011. (Clue – Ahmed plays for the country that will host the 2022 World Cup.)

Phil Jagielka in defensive action for

[   ] as he beats Zolt Gera in the air during the Wembley friendly match against [   ].

Tim Cahill is on duty for

_____ in

their Asian Cup match against

_____ .

Let's hope he got a free kick
because he is clearly being
fouled by Daiki Iwamasa!

Victor Anichebe is playing for

_____

here in a friendly against

_____ .

(Clue – Victor's opponents are the
world's largest producers of oil.)

Here's **Leighton Baines** in action

for _____

against _____

at Wembley in June 2011 in a European
Championship Group 6 qualifier that
ended in a 2-2 draw.

Wearing an unfamiliar number
seven jersey, **Seamus Coleman**
battles for possession for

_____

during their surprise 2-0
win against European giants

_____

in June 2011.

Marouane Fellaini
is playing for

_____

against

_____

here and he's trying to
win possession from
Cesc Fabregas.

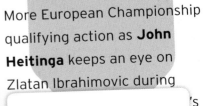

More European Championship
qualifying action as **John
Heitinga** keeps an eye on
Zlatan Ibrahimovic during

_____ 's

match against

_____ .

BELLEFIELD

Everton Football Club first started using Bellefield as a training base in 1946.

The place wasn't a full-time training ground though until the club modernised it in 1966. Situated in the West Derby area of Liverpool, some of greats of the English game sharpened their fitness on the pitches and in the gymnasiums at Bellefield – including Alan Ball, Alex Young, Joe Royle, Bob Latchford, Neville Southall, Dave Watson, Wayne Rooney and countless more.

Sadly though, as the 20th century gave way to the 21st, professional football was moving at a very rapid pace and after being classed as 'state-of-the-art' in 1966, Bellefield suddenly began to look tired and dated.

So, in 2007 Everton moved its training facility to the brand new, magnificent Finch Farm in the Halewood area of the city and Bellefield closed its gates for the last time.

The land on which Bellefield was built will now be re-developed for new houses and in March 2011 the bulldozers moved in and reduced the place to rubble...

SPOT THE DIFFERENCE

Can you spot the six differences between these photographs?

Answers on page 61

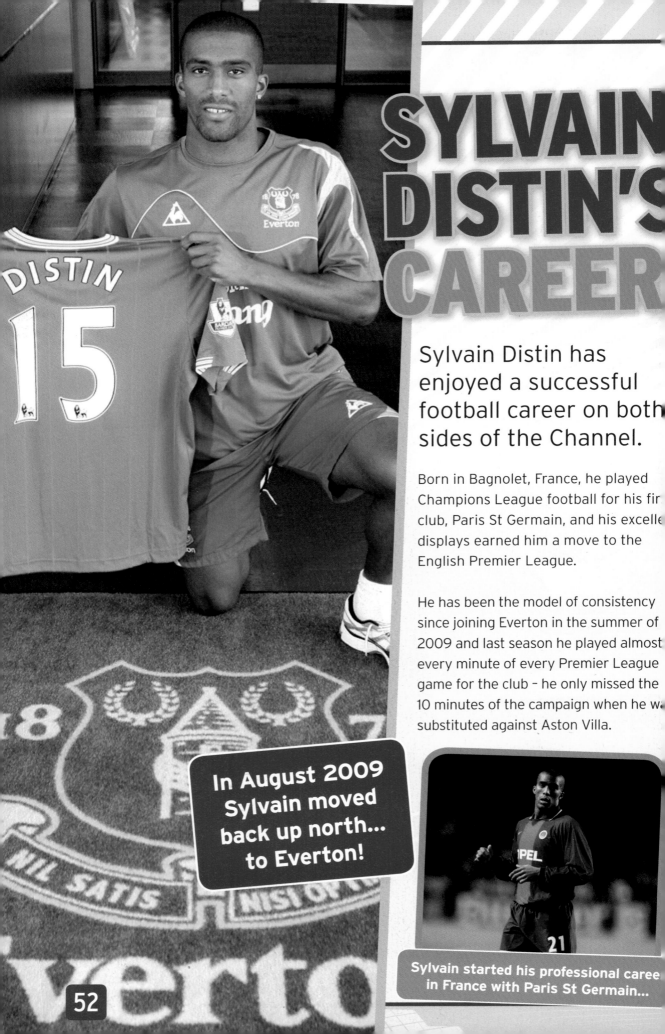

SYLVAIN DISTIN'S CAREER

Sylvain Distin has enjoyed a successful football career on both sides of the Channel.

Born in Bagnolet, France, he played Champions League football for his fir[st] club, Paris St Germain, and his excelle[nt] displays earned him a move to the English Premier League.

He has been the model of consistency since joining Everton in the summer of 2009 and last season he played almost every minute of every Premier League game for the club – he only missed the 10 minutes of the campaign when he w[as] substituted against Aston Villa.

In August 2009 Sylvain moved back up north... to Everton!

Sylvain started his professional caree[r] in France with Paris St Germain...

52

He was soon lured to the Premier League though and he joined ewcastle United on loan in 2001.

He made a permanent switch to England in 2002 when he signed for Manchester City.

In 2007, Sylvain moved to the south coast and teamed up with Harry Redknapp at Portsmouth.

Whilst with Pompey, Sylvain was an FA Cup final winner at Wembley in 2008.

His first goal for the club was in a uropa League tie against AEK Athens.

His most important goal was an equaliser against Liverpool in the Merseyside derby at Anfield in 2011.

DAD'S QUIZ

Q5

Q17

You'll probably need some help from a grown-up with this quiz! Or read the questions out and see if they score more than you did on the junior version..!!

1 Who is the only player to have won the FA Cup twice with Everton?

2 Who was Everton's assistant manager before Steve Round?

3 Against which team did Everton play their one and only European Champions League tie?

4 Who did Everton defeat 2-0 to secure their first Premier League win of last season?

5 Who did Everton defeat in the 3rd Round of the FA Cup last season?

6 Which other current Premier League team has Everton legend Joe Royle managed?

7 At Goodison Park, which stand is directly opposite the Park End?

8 Which Chinese company sponsored Everton before Chang Beer?

9 In the 2009 FA Cup semi-final penalty shot-out against Manchester United, who was the only Everton player to miss his kick?

10 What was Wayne Rooney's squad number at Everton?

11 For which other English club did Duncan Ferguson play?

12 Who were Everton's joint top-scorers last season?

13 Last season only two players played in every single Everton match in all competitions. Leighton Baines was one...who was the other?

14 What club links David Moyes, Thomas Gravesen and Alan Stubbs?

15 Which player has appeared more times in Europe for Everton than anyone else?

16 Who was the Everton Reserves team coach before Alan Stubbs?

17 Which Scottish team was former Everton striker Francis Jeffers playing for last season?

18 Name one of the two teams that Jermaine Beckford had loan spells at earlier in his career.

19 For which Premier League club have both Louis Saha and Sylvain Distin played?

20 Apart from Tim Cahill, who was the last Australian international to play for Everton?

Answers on **page 61**

TWO EVERTONS!

EVERTON 2
EVERTON 0
9:49 0:44

"There's Only One Everton!" sing the supporters...

Well, strictly speaking that's not completely true because as well as the Premier League club that we all know and love, there's also an Everton in the South American country of Chile!

CD Everton is based in the city of Viña del Mar and was founded in 1909 after a group of Anglo-Chilean teenagers formed a football club and named it after the Everton team that had just made a pioneering visit to South America.

The club is nicknamed 'Ruleteros' (roulette players) after Viña del Mar's status as a gambling resort.

Everton is Chile's sixth most successful team, having won the national title four times, and the club's home stadium is the 18,037 capacity Estadio Sausalito.

Everton (Chile) met Everton (England) for the very first time in the summer of 2010 in a friendly match at Goodison Park. It was a wonderful occasion with representatives from Chile absolutely delighted to be visiting the stadium for the very first time.
The English team won 2-0 and the scoreboard at Goodison Park that night, as you can see, was quite unique! The Toffees were then presented with the Copa Hermandad (known in English as the Brotherhood Trophy).

Ironically, the only time CD Everton have ever won the Chilean FA Cup was in 1984 – the same year that Everton won the English version for the fourth time! A group of enthusiastic Evertonians have formed a CD Everton Supporters' Society called The Ruleteros and they have been over to South America to watch the team in action.

For more information on the Chilean Everton and the Supporters' Society, visit
www.theruleteros.com

THE PLAYERS OF EVERTON...
AND EVERTON

55

LADIES IN EUROPE!

Everton have always prided themselves on doing well in European competitions – and it's not just the men's team!

The Everton Ladies continued their rapid progression by going all the way to the quarter finals of the European Champions League in the 2010/11 season.

Mo Marley's team travelled to all corners of Europe during their campaign, including stops in Lithuania, Hungary and Denmark.

The Ladies were particularly impressive in their three-game qualifying group – the Blues netted 23 goals without reply as they won all of their games at a canter.

That string of excellent performances sent the Blues into the knockout stages and they knew there were more difficult challenges ahead starting with MTK Hungaria in the round of 32.

The first leg was 0-0 but Everton romped home at Widnes in the return game... winning 7-1. Youngster Brooke Chaplen was the headline maker on a bitterly cold night, scoring a hat-trick.

TIM HOWARD AND RACHEL BROWN AT THE LAUNCH OF THE 2011 WOMEN'S SUPER LEAGUE

JILL SCOTT

EVERTON V DUISBURG IN THE EUROPEAN CHAMPIONS LEAGUE

In the next round Everton defeated highly rated Brondby 5-2 on aggregate to set up a quarter-final clash with the superb team from Germany, Duisburg.

The Germans were a great team and won both legs to end the European dream for The Blues, but it had been a brilliant adventure for the Ladies and they did the whole club proud with their efforts.

"It was a terrific run and we really enjoyed it," said manager, Mo Marley. "We've really put the name of Everton Ladies on the map and having had a taste of European football, the girls are desperate to do it again."

Everton Ladies are part of the 2011 Women's Super League - a brand new league created to help boost the profile of the female game.

The teams in the WSL are Arsenal Ladies, Birmingham Ladies, Bristol Academy, Chelsea Ladies, Doncaster Ladies, Everton Ladies, Lincoln Ladies and Liverpool Ladies.

Check **evertonfc.com** for the fixtures and go and support The Toffees!

EVERTON STRIKER NATASHA DOWIE

NAME THAT

PLAYER

How well do you know the Premier League footballers?

Here are 19 pictures of players who played in the Premier League last season (one from each club ... apart from Everton!) See how many of them you can name.

Write your answers on a sheet of paper, time yourself to see how long it takes you to name them all and then test your friends to see if they can beat you!

Answers on **page 61**

JAGS THE GOALIE!

Phil Jagielka's performances at the heart of the Everton defence have been terrific since he joined the club from Sheffield United in 2007.

Indeed, the popular centre-half is now a regular fixture in the England squad – but how many Evertonians are aware that during his professional career, Jags has played in goal FOUR times?

JAGS CONCENTRATES BETWEEN THE STICKS

… AND CELEBRATES A FAMOUS WIN

During his time at Sheffield United, Jags showed so much natural ability between the sticks in training that his manager, Neil Warnock, opted not to have a goalkeeper as one of his substitutes – opting instead to put Jags in whenever the goalie got injured or sent-off!

"I have always been half-decent in goal," said the Blues star.

"It goes back to when I was six or seven and my older brother Steve would stick me in there and fire shots at me. I'm pretty athletic and agile, I guess, and that obviously helps."

Jags' finest afternoon as an emergency goalkeeper came against Arsenal in December 2006 when he kept goal for an hour…and kept a clean sheet!

So does he think that David Moyes will ever ask him to take the gloves for a Premier League game at Goodison Park? "I doubt it!" he laughed. "The gaffer wouldn't dare take the risk!"

QUIZ ANSWERS

SPOT THE DIFFERENCE Page 51

PLAYER PROFILES Page 14-19

Howard-Two: Hibbert-FA Youth Cup: Baines-he missed: Distin-AEK Athens: Jagielka-The Blades: Heitinga-Uruguay: Bilyaletdinov-Man Utd: Osman-Macclesfield: Coleman-Blackpool: Cahill-true: Rodwell-Sigma Olomouc: Fellaini-Morocco: Neville-Wolves: Saha-Beckford: Anichebe-UEFA Cup

JUNIOR QUIZ Page 20

1)Sligo Rovers; 2)Russia; 3)1995; 4) Brentford; 5)Celtic; 6)younger; 7)Distin and Beckford; 8)Huddersfield and Scunthorpe; 9)Leeds; 10)Dixie Dean; 11) Walter Smith; 12)Millwall; 13)France; 14)5; 15)Philadelphia Union and DC United; 16) Nigeria; 17)Marouanne Fellaini; 18)1987; 19) Diniyar Bilyaletdinov; 20)They all play for USA

SPONSORS Page 21

1) Manchester United; 2) Arsenal; 3) Chelsea; 4) Manchester City; 5) Newcastle United

WORDSEARCH Page 36

HAT-TRICK HEROES Page 42-43

Yakubu-SK Brann; Watson-Leeds United; Campbell-West Ham; Ferguson-Bolton; Sharp-Sheffield Wednesday; Lineker-Birmingham City

EVERTON INTERNATIONALS Page 48-49

Bilyaletdinov-Russia v Qatar; Jagielka-England vs Hungary; Cahill-Australia v Japan; Anichebe-Nigeria v Saudi Arabia; Baines-England v Switzerland; Coleman-Republic of Ireland v Italy; Fellaini-Belgium v Spain; Heitinga-Holland v Sweden

DAD'S QUIZ Page 54

1)Neville Southall; 2) Alan Irvine; 3) Villarreal; 4) Birmingham; 5) Scunthorpe; 6) Manchester City; 7) Gwladys Street; 8) Kejian; 9) Tim Cahill; 10) 18; 11) Newcastle; 12) Beckford and Cahill; 13) Tim Howard; 14) Celtic; 15) Tony Hibbert; 16) Andy Holden; 17) Motherwell; 18) Scunthorpe and Carlisle; 19) Newcastle; 20) Lucas Neill

NAME THAT PLAYER Page 58-59

Top row (left to right) – Kevin Doyle (Wolves), Rory Delap (Stoke), Phil Bardsley (Sunderland)
Middle Row (left to right) – Andy Johnson (Fulham), Darren Bent (Aston Villa), Florent Malouda (Chelsea), Kevin Davies (Bolton), Cameron Jerome (Birmingham), Jason Roberts (Blackburn), Ali Al-Habsi (Wigan), Alex Song (Arsenal)
Bottom Row (left to right) – John Flanagan (Liverpool), Scott Carson (West Brom), Scott Parker (Aston Villa), Michael Dawson (Tottenham), David Silva (Manchester City), Charlie Adam (Blackpool), Shola Ameobi (Newcastle), Antonio Valencia (Manchester United)

EVERTON FC

62